My West

Jenifer Fox

ISBN:979-8-9868389-6-0

Published by Quillkeepers Press, LLC
PO Box 10236
Casa Grande, AZ 85130

*For Christopher and Mary Wheeler
for encouraging me to keep writing.*

Contents

Evidence

God hoped
we'd write poetry.
You know how I know?
Pomegranates.
Antioxidants aside,
their purpose as a mere fruit is questionable.
Bananas, watermelon, pineapples- all understandable.
Even the Brazilian nut is worth the effort
given the size of the prize,
though seemingly overprotective.
But the pomegranate!
The design is intended to provoke
for who cannot see
  the coaxing red of the leathery rind,
  protecting the blood-plump rubies
  blushing beneath the white linen sheet
as anything but subject matter?

My mother gave me my first pomegranate
as a 13th birthday gift.
No explanation.

Those were the years I wrote poems
for comfort
to save
the smallest piece of me.

I was too young to write of fertility,
fervor, forbidden fruit.

Instead, I wrote
the seeds seemed packed in like a jumbo jet headed to Mardi Gras.
Then waited for God to smile.

A Child Copes

The cracked egg lay on the cement
baby blue pieces of fallen sky
the day my mother first went away
and she'd disapprove of the way I touched it
like the 100-year-old teacup, I shattered
before knowing how fragile
things can break and won't be put back together.

It must have been the wind,
                (all that power we can't see)
that knocked it from the nest. Curious
carrion, most peculiar creature—
a bruise without bones still
moist in the yolk,
all rubbery beak and purple membrane
curled in a fetal ball.

The red-breasted hen was nowhere.
Hopeless,
she'd left the featherless
thing to wither.

With no one to scold me
I lifted the teaspoonful of keratin,
cradled it in my little-bird hand
for the briefest moment. The bizarre

beginning of loving things already gone
and holding fast to something broken.

Ephemeral

Autumn approaches in the distance,
grief-smoke of pinon rides in on the wind.
Small comfort for inevitable loss.
Another summer vanishes,
slips away in silence
without saying good-bye.

Fire licks September's edges
yellow, orange, red
flare deep in leaf-veins.
Maple, aspen, elm
ignite ambivalent blaze.
Why is it I feel sorrow
whenever something leaves?

By October,
each day outdoes the last.
At its apex it's downright
excruciating.
Ephemeral flame
like a promise we know will be broken
but we believe it anyway.

With sweatered limbs
I hug the barrel of bluebird sky
high on incense-air
the world too brilliant to bear

like the spark of first love
knowing it will burn
but we strike the match anyway.

I hear
the rustle of my destiny.

Tomorrow,
there will be storm clouds
and the trees begin to bare
their cold arms.

Ambiguous Loss

Bloodline threads us together.
My aunt and I

walk along the Rio Grande.
Somehow, we'd both migrated south
released from history, the ancestors frozen in place.

Stories flow between us
while somewhere above,

a clamor startles us. We stop
and search the sky.
                    Cranes
                    from the marshes of Wisconsin,
the grey state of our   escape.

The flock turns toward sunlight,
white robe flashes against blue absolute.

     Ciseaux on thermals, a magic trick, mesmerizes
until an errant wind bothers a whole line of cottonwoods.

The tiny applause draws our attention.
When we look up again,   the air is empty
                    of any expectation they'll return.

II.
Loss isn't a story. Untethered
                    to chronology, it resists closure
like a New Mexico winter:
        blizzard in late October,
        followed by a month of sunshine.
        Scant dusting Christmas Eve,
        fallow January, power
        outages in February, March
        a lamb.   Windstorms
        in April.   Ambiguous,
        messy accumulation.

How the first snowfall may be too heavy to lift.
The backwards glance of the vestigial storm.

It takes a whole life span to stand back and make sense of it all.

Three paw prints preserved in plaster on my bookshelf.
I carry the remains of life's losses from place to place to place.

III.
The snow is suddenly weeping. The air damp with hope.
Love lived briefly in the dry spaces
                        between new beginnings.

Whale Watching at Night

The Sturgeon Moon rose
like an offering to the sky

from the pregnant waters of the Salish Sea
in the summer I became nobody,

the summer of my last menses,
which may have been a loss,

but according to Darwin, I'd been useless all along.

On the shore of Saturna Island,
with forty years ahead of me, I waited, extant.

I waited, impatient and simmering, the soup
before boil, hot.

I waited, unnoticed, up to my ankles in sand,
while the waves washed me in salt and magnesium.

I expected to find what I'd earned
through half a lifetime dragging behind me

this hollow habit of healing.

In the glance between diving in
and turning away, I spotted them,

slick glide through moonbeams,
the dorsal fins sliced the surface.

I'd waited all week to spot an Orca.

Soul-sharing matriarch,
midway between birth and death,

she, too, evolved for menopause.
She, too, fit for greater survival.

The pause that separates feeling from thinking—

in that moment—sudden breach, she broke through

the surface, ballooned into the air,
flashed against the darkness,
fluke like arms outstretched, she spun,

and every atom in me, a crescendo

pulsating until she slapped the surface—
                then disappeared.

The sun rose. I danced.

55 No Limit

A thousand-year-old fortune
teller quivered
as she traced the crease
across the blushing face of my outstretched palm.
Your lifeline is long
but broken.

That was decades ago,
Jackson Square, New Orleans.

I rolled my eyes, then drifted
toward oysters and champagne.

Today, I am 55 years old.
On the back road to Abiquiu,
I pass the sign:
Speed, 55.
Refusing regulation,
I jamb down the clutch,
shift upward,
and launch into the Jemez Mountains.
No destination, no regrets.

I grip the steering wheel—
(Five fingers right side,
five fingers left), I am twisted
juniper let go of rock ledge,
rough ride in the shadow of Ghost Ranch,
pilgrim of possibility I power past
the broken part.

I am a high priestess,
pulse beat in the promised land.

Where I Belong

The canyon rises
raspberry ribbon layers,
a cake baked in the oven
of the noonday sun.
Lavender ledges
stacked against
the blue sheet
impossible sky.
100 million years
etched in ancient seawall.
Deltas return to dust.
Everything evaporates,
loses form and becomes
something new
and unrecognizable.
Rusted cliff face bleeds
into crystalline river.
Rock returns to water.
This is the place
of my everything,
where my heart sings
desert song:
fire, water, earth, sun.
The place where I belong.

My West

It's my West, too,
this place of sandstone spires
and boundless sky.

My paint and brushes speak something true.

No swaggering sheriffs or lonely outlaws.
No need for Navajos
wrapped in oil-shined blankets
pretentiously peaceful,
as though we didn't destroy
every. last. one.

No clean covered wagons brimming with copper pots.
No steely-eyed fur trappers
scouting petroglyph canyons.
Just sage-coated ridge tops,
swashes of open space,   room enough
for a woman's view.

It's baffling how stagnant macho tropes
still raise the auction paddle and oversell
the appropriated dystopia
of mass-produced boys.

Hasn't anyone told them
the Marlboro Man has bad breath,
there's more stretch than denim in his 501's,
Broncos, Mustangs, and Range Rovers
are just cars?

Oh, by the way,
women mended fences, too.
Scorpions and snakes
saw them coming and slid under rocks for cover.

Apricot blossoms dance through the valley.
No cowboys necessary.

La Jicarita Mountain

Little bowl wrought upon the slow wheel of time,
you shaped the Pecos wilderness, a once-full cup,

you poured into the valley and gave rise
to corn, melons, beans, feathers, skins

the sustenance of survival for generations
of Archuleta, Martinez, Medina, and Picuris

who lived beneath you, pinched mica pots
for chicharrónes roasted above an open fire,

history now crumbling and pockmarked.
Now half-full, upside down, emptying,

your timbers lost to the railroads,
your water clogged and diverted—La Jicarita,

it will take many lifetimes to refill you.
How long does a mountain wait?

Fishing the Rio del Pueblo

Summer folds in half
and I roll around in the crease
like some wild berry
still ripe but off the vine.
I find my way

to the water's edge
where I become reed thin
stripped of all pretenses
the only way to receive
what I desire.

I pause,
wet foot steadied
beneath chalk-dry branch
never noticed by
a human eye before
mine. A black fly lands
on my finger. I don't flick
it away.

The art of anything
begins with reverence.

The forest rustles as I struggle
with the filament
thin, translucent as angel hair
while the size-16
elk hair caddis
eyehole waits
sturdy and open.
And for the third time,
stubborn refusal.

Everything now depends
on exactitude, laser focus
absolute reduction-
the one true test of the day.
Exquisite belief in the smallest fête
like the day I added and subtracted
then walked away. How difficult
these seemingly simple
decisions to go or stay.

Patience is the only way in,
even as the wind steals
the gossamer line from my fingers
and tosses it to the mouth of a hungry breeze.
Devil's feast returns bones,
a tangled snarl. Penance
for a life of haste.

The mountains loom like judges,
She'll give up.
They turn a shade of lavender.

I accept the conditions of success
and where others quit
I stay with the catechism of the knots.

Finally,
the Sweet Timothy lifts its fragrance,
the nuthatch harmonizes with the stream's riffle,
the line cooperates— eases through the knot
the fly agrees,
the river expands and lets me in.

All streaks and flashes now—
Unison is nature's way.

Then
tug!
rod up, hook set
rainbow glistens as it turns toward the sky.

There you go, now take your prize.

The fish,
the one that waited for me.

Pot Brownies

At the art opening
a pair of Taos sorceresses
enchanted guests with Alice B. Toklas brownies
and failed to tell us.

It was minutes
or   maybe   a few hours   some time
definitely   later
eve   ry
thin   g
turn-
          ed al l
                    Pic   a   sso.

I melted   across   the snow-   cover
          ed town

                    amplified   ***** drenched in !!!!! frequencies
sparkling in the star-gorged night

utterly checked in

I stood on the ledge of the Rio Grande
my mind,
                              still sparking peculiar.

The river wound serpentine
below the canyon's rim
                         and from her silver back, a mist
lifted   sojourners' voices

they thundered   HALLELUJAHS
through a thousand winters past.

That is when I finally   lost it.

Everything shapeshifted.
My body dissolved glitter, granite, chaotic, wizardry.

Finally, something happened to me.

I am brand new
awakened from stagnant sleep.

Taos Mountain

Sentient, she is crowned by the morning
star. Proud daughter of the sun,
sovereign minister to the moon,
legend has it, she will welcome
or spit you out. But I know

it's the depth of the dream
or the width of the wound
that determines whether she'll open
or shut.

Beneath her shadow, I release
foreboding joy and slip
through the narrow eye
of the needle
where I am free to paint
new meaning into the days
of my plein air life
among common saints
and unconscious sinners,
whose sufferings wrought me alive.

First breath beyond the silent past
the mountain's rocks wait
to cry out.

She is an exalted landscape
and I am a portrait
in repose
knowing I belong
to her permanent collection,
an eternity that outlasts death.

Uncharted Territory

Dusk settles the restless day
into half-tones.

I sit beside you
on broken stones worn smooth with time

hoping it's not too late
to finally see and be seen.

Skin barely brushing skin,
our breath aligns.

No nervous conversation,
superficial bonding
over people and places we didn't share,
like children or first homes,
the years spent beside another.
We explore new love in old bodies
having earned the right to be worshipped.

This isn't starting over, nobody's been here before.

Darkness creeps across the black chalk
canyon wall eclipsing sunbeams
still clinging to the surface.
Shadows reveal
new forms
as the day ends and
we begin.

Last Love

Yesterday,
we discovered a high mountain field
draped in daisies,
laced and laid out like a wedding dress,
woven with dew-drenched cobwebs,
undaunted, yet, modest,
like love that lasts.

Later,
I lay alone in the blackbird night
beneath creaking cottonwoods,
the stream babbled incoherent.
I clenched brittle grass,
yanked it from the head of the earth.
Something to hold onto.

Today,
braiding your fingers through mine,
you weave the earth and sky together.
First touch.
Unadulterated love
planted before frost.
Guarantee of another spring.

Brave Hereafter

At the Pueblo, we collect photos on the shortest day of the year—
40th anniversary of the accident he won't mention.
Kivas with blue doors, second story ladders propping the past—
stretched-skin drums, a few dreamcatchers, turquoise trinkets.

Abundance of red willows shiver along the sacred
stream,
clouds loom like ghosts,
shadows lengthen broken arrows
across the southwest corner cemetery.
Plot of land no one can steal.

Forefathers, grandfathers, governors, chiefs,
their hallowed names crumble from tombstone faces.

Silence swells between us.
You'd think the dead would speak more loudly
to the soul-severed sons they left behind.

It's an annual ceremony of forgetting
the ones who never came home
but still hang around
just beyond the thin veil of evening.

Faint beats, soft-footed dancers.
The whisper-rituals of permanent loss.
The suddenness of death that shatters through history
taking down one hollow year after another
while lonely and lost
the little boy beside the grave
abruptly became a man.
Hereafter, brave imitator.

It's dark by time we reach the chapel.
I take his wintered hand,
slip it into my pocket.

To Love a Landscape Painter

Between brush strokes,
the painter steps back,

reframes his options,
searches for a shadow,

then punishes himself.
The language of dawn

seep through his hands,
as he spreads feverish sunlight

across cold stone ledges,
daubs reverence into every rock

They know him here
where skeletons shelter

and spiders weave blankets
on maple looms, edging

twig, leaf, and tendril.
His place is among the ruins,

historian of a collapsing past,
he listens to clay that crumbles

wanting to be something more
than a home.

I slip into his sweater,
notice three specks of yellow paint,

the moment I knew
I loved him.

The Last Superpower

Autumn, 2018
in the year of alternative facts

we are raw-nerved and disoriented,
so me, my man, and dog cruise

across America in an RV
before it's too late

to feast on something sublime.
We crave the whole bucketful.

Stuffing ourselves with super-sized sunsets,
we slurp down venti vistas, gorge

on canyons, licking at ice caps.
We devour the extra-large landscapes

that might or (I might as well say it)
might not hold tomorrow.

We skip Las Vegas. We've already won.
We binge on second chances.

Nevada feels sovereign, full-bellied
statesman spread out naked

and unashamed, barebacked
mountains, fat with missiles.

The rivers are thirsty.
When there's nothing left to swallow,

the earth will spit us out.
We rattle down the loneliest highway

together — between Utah and California
we rise into the open jaw

of the Sierras
as the last Superpower belches.

Desire

I want you
to see me
the way that one rare brush of yellow
makes the whole painting come alive.
Then, as if you've never tried before,
I want you to wipe your eyes
and begin again,
this time, not worrying
if anyone will think it good
or not.
Just wet the bristle
and lay me down
in the quickening.
Lean into what is essential.
Let it be a marriage
of complementary colors.
Capture me
in shapes and shadows.
Toss me effortlessly across the canvas
until you are bewitched by your own talent
and I am pulsating purple
and glowing orange.

Make the World Magic Again

We wanted strangeness
redwoods   falling
                        upwards
communion with bees   draped in tiger fur jackets
minding their own business
                        eating atoms
We were alive and buzzing free.

When she said *xertz*, we fell to the ground   amazed
her mouth gaping wide as a mushroom moon
star teeth circling   her serpent tongue
unregulated   laughter, natural   happiness
as if 2016 never happened.

When they dipped their hands in mud
                        we melted into something sacred
                        shimmered through the woods
golden auras
                        stripped down   to essential   softness.
It took six hours to land again
back to a world more fearful
        less magic.
Returning, eyes to usual form
we sat on the park-bench
and wept.

Replacement

Side-by-side
we crouch on the curb
tow truck on the way
a bag of sunflower seeds
is all we have left
to share.

I split a seed with the arrow of my eye tooth,
lay the shell in the crease between sidewalk squares
wonder how far   it strayed
from becoming a sunflower.

You launch yours with a dart of your tongue,
a technique, I suspect,
perfected by years
of French kissing and holding back
important words.

Content with small talk,
you repeat stories from your past
as though you don't know me.

I spot a white-throated sparrow
side eyeing me from across the street   he covets our snack
mechanically tilts his head
ruffles and hops   closer.

I toss a handful his way
the exact moment the words sprout from your mouth,
This is all your fault.
Anything for a reaction.

The sparrow snatches the nearest seed
the next,   the next   and the next.
Next,
I'm sure of this,
the bird will be eating from my hand
making a nest in my hair
chirping soft melodies.

But the tow truck arrives, and it's time for me to speak.
Can it be fixed?
It depends on what you're willing to put into it.

What's Left

A lone coyote tiptoes toward the door.
An opportunist,

he runs off with the dog's bone,
glisten of fat and grizzle in moonlight.

A pair of crows argue
between trees. They are jealous

the hummingbirds sucked the feeder dry
before soaring south.

Bears, desperate, pillage
trash bins, scatter empty

bean cans across the driveway.
Flee the scene.

In bed, you face the wall.
Sunlight breaks

through curtains, casts a shadow
between us. A suitcase waits at the door.

The Way It Ends

The snow didn't melt
the year I turned 50. A year
I didn't have to spare.
In the winter of my lifetime,
ice blue text bubble ends
half a decade without good-bye.

My lover's departure froze
me in place. January-March, fossilized. I was trapped

in young woman's despair, wounded
with no time to heal.

In the months it took to thaw
my friends became mothers-of-the-bride
had grandchildren
some even died.

I wish I never learned
that hoover is more than a vacuum
love bombs, trauma triggers, wound bonded,
lessons learned on Tic Tok at 3:00AM.

I never saw it coming.

Unnecessary and cold.
At our age
leaving should include lending a sweater,
a hot cup of coffee,
a week's worth of calling
to see if I'm ok.

I'm not ok.
Now I believe in ghosts
that haunt me with clocks.
Another milestone missed. Another door
that never closes.

Confetti

The day you shredded me,
rolled down the window of your dented truck,
pitched   me
                                    to   the wind,
left me
                      scattered   in the dust
of your worn tires,

I might have cried,
Had a rush of wind not   lifted me.
Confetti catching sunlight,
                                          I flowed in every direction.
My petal-pieces new-found friends,
pleasing
   fields,   forests,   and flowerbeds.
Come nightfall, you'd regret it.
By then, *He never existed.*
By then, it would be impossible to
put it back together
and hold me
in such a tiny hand.

The Dark Place

that day you open your eyes
but don't wake up
the ton of bricks
so neatly netted
to the far corner
of your little sky
rains down on
       you   buried in the bottomless bed
             accept the blows
it doesn't matter
       you   curled in hum drum stupor
             dissolve into chaos accept
                captivity

day waits outside the window   indifferent
shapes collapse   then merge to beige
words, wisps of smoke in the windless room
the faucet
     with a slow
     drip
     dries
friends and family call
already muted   you don't pick up
little lost thing
engulfed in sullen fog
no mother can save you
riveted to pain you lay beside yourself
      speechless
abyss squanders weeks   maybe months
the purloined days have forfeited their names
it no longer matters

why this happened
elusive loss   triggers   bleak flashes
hidden in the fertile
          past   tense
where sadness was a gentle muse

Apparently, you needed something fiercer.

And if you're reading this
in the warmth of the redeeming sun,
you understand
how even the tiniest glimmer of light
can prick darkness.
Slightest variance—   the shadow that reached back
when you offered your hand.
You felt the feint pulse of faith.
Words, like moths on the long tongue of a Venus
Slipper, return.
Velvet-winged transfer,
                              it was the body
that saved you
when it opened to grace.

Unbroken Circle

At the Grief Center,
I unfold
an aluminum chair and squeeze into the morning
group, listening to shattering stories of loss.
I wonder where I fit in.

Beside me, a mother.
Her 12-year-old, thrown from the car in a head-on
three years to the day.
Next to her, he shares
how his wife, rotted from cancer, died
a week before their 20th wedding
anniversary.

The stories advance clockwise
until they circle
unbroken back to me.

What's your story?

I inhale
then confess
I've never been wholly
loved
Eyes widen, foreheads crinkle.
I bore no children.
They lean toward me, waiting
for a death that didn't unravel.
I hold back tears.

I am a full breast
with no mouth to feed
an unlit candle
for nobody's birthday
the book with the ending ripped out
lost pages
no anniversaries
no visits to tombstones
no before and after
just the dark shadow mourning
for things that never were.

Heart Song

I remember the song of my heart.
It bleeds first
then sings in the mending.

Amazing grace
Holy, holy, holy
The unconditional melody
of better angels

Desert Rock

The Chama Canyon is a rock
and roll stadium concert.
I am buried in the audience
general admission, lawn tickets
where Winter's bitter breath
can't find me.
That bitch nearly broke me.

Here to heal.
I shake with the hard-driving beat of the rapids
rattle with rockslide electric shredding rifts
roll with the harmonies of ten thousand wrens
tumble through layers of morning.
Boogie-woogie rocking pneumonia on the riverbank.

Late afternoon atmosphere
settles into mellow spiccato.
Quaking Aspens rustle wind chimes
percussion solo in the quicksilver twilight.

Bonfire intermission.
I lay down and rest.

Laser light show comet-streaked sky
coyote sharp-pitched soloist
steady pulse of high-country backbeat
stars, a million lighters waving
Encore, Encore!
I am released and shaken clean.

Yellow Chrysanthemums

Late November, evening
is an interruption
in barren yard
full of rubble and scratches.

I wait for relief—
snowfall.

Lazy sun licks the valley pewter,
casts pale rays on the aluminum barrel, empty
stalks now tanned and brittle.
Chrysanthemums,
their close-grown stems
now twisted, bare.
I tighten my scarf

as the last light illuminates
the hard-polished day,
and remember

the buoyant yellow buds,
early August, the golden days

of their—of our—blossoming.

Memory,
beautiful and tender.

The bloom that never dies.

Queen of the Andes

In the waiting room,
I leaf through *Discover* magazine,
and land on an article about the Puya Raimondii,
the world's largest bromeliad,
cousin to the pineapple,
a plant geek's dream.

Plant that Eats Birds
Provocative headline.
I cling to the cover when the nurse calls my name.

My eyes still pinned to the page,
she straps the blood-pressure cuff to my arm,

holds a thermometer gun to my head,

clips a pulse meter to my finger.

Queen of the Andes
Towers 50-feet
Survives 100-years
in arid, hardscrabble land
blooms once in its lifetime
near the very end
bears 8,000 white flowers,
containing six million seeds,
then quickly dies.

I lift the photo for the nurse:
White flowers at the tips of each horn-shaped branch.

52

When's the last time you menstruated?
I dig deep for the memory of blood,
a loss I didn't grieve.
I've forgotten how to count backward
past the long, loveless stretch,
through all the absences I traveled.
Twenty years.
All life's possibilities now finite.
She tightens the band above my elbow,
turns my palm upward, taps my wrist,
jabs the needle into blue vein rush of red.
I feel my own glory rising.
A great flowering awaits.
What have you eaten today?
Birds.

Salvation

      might be

the buffalo head   thundercloud

      gliding across the turquoise sky   before

colliding with the cowboy   hat cumulus

at the precise moment

you reach for me

and I know this is

enough.

Narrative

Old people tell stories
young people no longer read.
I accept that
rejection
acknowledge the confrontation
you believe   bonded to narrative,
I've regressed
accepted the ease of suicide
lingered too long on the distance from there   to here.

Before you were born,
I lost days in search of a single phrase
whole mornings on my knees
reaching for one right word
picked off places, killed characters
held a mirror to your hunger for jouissance.

Before long, we'll all be gone.

Fire doesn't lie.
Water won't resist.
Air refuses capture.
Light denies darkness.

Gravity delights in propping us up while holding us down.

Voice speaks truth—we listen
Diction drives context —we believe
Syntax suggests music —we surrender
Structure offers connection—we unite

Words confer power while taking it away.

By the dint of our anchor
we paw our way toward meaning
too late for imprint
when the shadows, having paid their debt,
erase our existence
we will return without trace
to primordial silence
the place before all this horror
where we will float unbound.

Water trickles down the acequia.
Jobs vanish.
Dogs die.
Love lost.
Innocence stolen.
Mountain forgives.
Loss marries joy.

Something simple remains—
The good things.
A well-lived life.
The wound inside the pomegranate.
Daughter/woman rising toward revolt of abject despair.
Mother to these anxious words,
I reach with the grasping hand of a laughing child,
for the one thing
God hoped for...

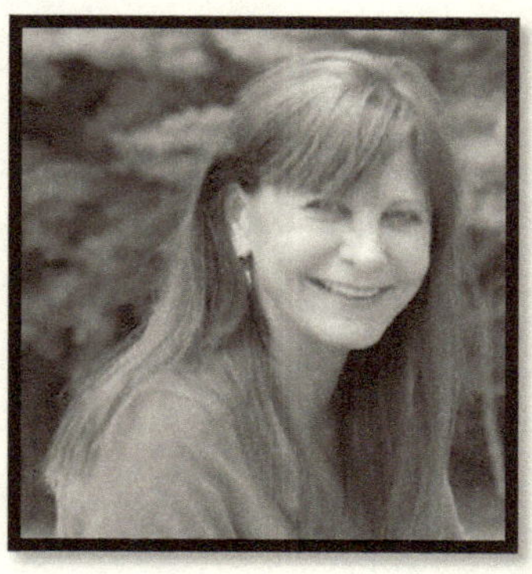

Jenifer Fox was born and raised in Milwaukee, Wisconsin. She holds degrees from The University of Wisconsin-Madison, The Bread Loaf School of English, and Harvard University. She is also the author of *Your Child's Strengths* (Viking/Penguin) and *The Differentiated Instruction Book of Lists* (Jossey-Bass). After a noteworthy career as an educator, Jenifer now resides in Taos, New Mexico, where she works as a full-time writer and watercolor artist. Her poems Fishing the Rio Del Pueblo and La Jicarita won first and second place, respectively, in the 2020 Southwestern Poet's Society annual literary awards competition. In addition, her paintings have been shown in galleries throughout the United States and featured in literary magazines.